You Can Do That?

Amazing People
with
Amazing Jobs

by David Messick
Original Illustrations by
Liu Light and Alvin Septiawan

You Can Do <u>That?</u>

Amazing People with Amazing Jobs

© 2021 / All Rights Reserved

By David Messick

Original Children Illustrations by Lucia Liu

Original Chapter Page Illustrations by Alvin Septiawan

Puppet Images Rainbow Productions, Inc.

Designed by Lynn Mangosing and Jasmine Racy

ISBN: 987-1-73-324845-7

Second printing / Printed in the USA

Rainbow Puppet Publications 18 Easthill Court, Hampton, Virginia 23664

Rainbow Puppet Productions is a non-profit, educational entertainment company

Thanks to

Traci Massie, Erin Matteson, Curtis Johnson and Optima Health
Tony Gabriele, Robin McCormick, David & Stephanie Messick, Marcy Messick,
Nancy Kent Swilley, and Rose West

Back Cover photos by Marcy Messick, Blackbeard Pirate Festival,
Hampton, VA (Hampton CVB), David Messick, and
Chris Mangune – Visual Artistry Media

Dedicated to the puppet makers
who helped me find my
dream job...

Craig T. Adams, Fiona Andrews, Laura Baldwin, Kathie Davis,
Chris Frank, Jill Harrington, Frank Lakus, Stephanie Messick,
Regina Smith, Helen Spaetzel, and Jason Wiedel

Contents:

"Believe you can and you're halfway there."

Teddy Roosevelt

Introduction

Rainbow Puppet Productions just finished our busiest season of shows ever. Our tour took us to many preschools, schools, and libraries that we had never visited before.

While the locations ranged from small indoor classrooms to large outdoor events, we noticed that one thing remained the same. At almost every event we could count on fans in t-shirts featuring mermaids, pirates, unicorns, dinosaurs, rocket ships, rainbows, monster trucks, alligators, and other creepy creatures. It's no wonder that our pirate show remains so

Piirate puppet.
(Rainbow Puppets)

popular and our mermaid gets more fan mail than all of our other puppets combined! She's only onstage for 20 seconds in our current show and still gets hundreds of letters and drawings.

Mermaid puppet. (Rainbow Puppets)

That's how I came to write this book. What would it be like to ride on a unicorn or a monster truck or a rocket ship? What would it be like to touch a rainbow or build a dinosaur or stare down an alligator? What would it be like to really be a mermaid or a pirate? Well, there's no need to dream about it... I found out the answer to each of these questions and I'm happy to share what I learned.

That Face! Blackbeard

Of all the pirates that ever roamed the seas perhaps the most famous was Blackbeard the Pirate. Sailing with his crew, up and down the Atlantic Coast, his reputation alone could send fear and dread to sea-farers and land-lovers alike. He once held the port of Charleston, South Carolina, hostage and got all that he was after without firing a single shot.

Those lucky enough to survive a battle with Blackbeard would tell stories of a loud and fearless captain. Above all, most would remember that face... That scary face, those piercing eyes, and that beard that appeared to be fire. Legend has it he would put candles under his hat to create a smoky effect.

Blackbeard. (Pixabay)

Blackbeard went from success to success until a battle in Ocracoke, North Carolina, in 1718, when his luck left him. He didn't go quickly. It took 22 gunshots and five swipes of a sword to end his career. Even after his death, that face remained as a warning to other pirates. His head was hung in the harbor of Hampton, Virginia, as a clear message: pirates aren't welcome here.

MEET BEN CHERRY

Blackbeard Pirate Festival, Hampton, VA. (Hampton CVB)

It's a thrilling and terrifying sight... all at the same time. Standing by the waterfront in Hampton, Virginia, cannon blasts warn you that the ship headed to dock is here for serious business. Then you see him... the pirate captain in all his glory. He wears a huge pirate hat. There are red bows tied into his long black beard. This isn't just any pirate captain. It's the captain of all pirate captains. It's Blackbeard... returning to Hampton to avenge his name. It's hard to believe that the very city that hung his head on a pole in the port entryway is now honoring the pirate with his own annual festival.

Of course, this Blackbeard has not really returned from the dead, he is the creation of a gifted performer named Ben Cherry. The performer brings decades of pirate experience to his portrayal, having appeared as the noted captain from New York all the way to Key West, Florida.

Ben was born in Darden, North Carolina. His father owned the local appliance store but encouraged Ben's interest in theater. Ben got a degree from East Carolina University, which fittingly sports a pirate as the school mascot. He then headed off to Broadway and New York City where he dated a Radio City Rockette and secured a job at NBC studios at Rockefeller Center. As a page for "Jeopardy!" and the "Tonight Show with Johnny Carson," he got to meet many of the most famous and influential people who came to the studio in the late 1960's and early 1970's. He was most impressed to meet the Apollo 11 astronauts after they completed the first human landing on the moon.

The "Tonight Show" eventually moved to Los Angeles, California, and Ben returned to North Carolina to help run his family's appliance store. Ben actually became a real-life Maytag repairman but he still dreamed of acting.

The town of Bath, North Carolina, would provide the answer to Ben's dream. Bath was home to Mary Ormond, one of 14 women alleged to have been married

Blackbeard Pirate Festival, Hampton, VA. (Hampton CVB)

to Edward Teach. If you haven't heard of Edward Teach, by now you've certainly heard his other name... Blackbeard the Pirate. Bath decided to recognize their notorious former resident with an outdoor drama called "Blackbeard's Knights of the Black Flag" and Ben was cast in the lead role.

While the play eventually ended, Cherry's love of the character did not. His long black beard and broad facial expressions made him the perfect person to portray the pirate.

Ben says, "Blackbeard was a great actor. I suspect he was a greater actor than he was a pirate. He understood that he needed to put on a great show. From the way he dressed to the ribbons in his beard… he was larger-than-life."

Blackbeard Pirate Festival, Hampton, VA. (Hampton CVB)

Unwilling to give up that larger-than-life character, Ben created a one-man show about Blackbeard. With the help of his wife, Dee Gee, he has taken the show to hundreds of schools, festivals, and events.

Along the way, he has become a celebrity. He has been featured in Smithsonian Magazine and many other publications. His advice to anyone who wishes to portray a historic character: "Make sure you really enjoy the character. You'll need to spend a lot of time studying their lives. If you're successful, you'll spend even more time portraying that character."

That's certainly true for Ben Cherry. He's going on over 40 years as Blackbeard the Pirate.

MEET CINDY KAYS

Yes, there are female pirates. Some are quite well known.

In 1700's America, Anne Bonny left her pirate husband John Bonny to follow the more famous pirate "Calico Jack." She disguised herself as a man and served as his first mate on the ship Revenge. When the crew was captured, it was Ann's pregnancy that kept her from being hanged with the other pirates.

In China in 1807, Cheng I Sao took over as leader of one of the largest bands of pirates in history when her husband died. The gang had hundreds of ships and tens of thousands of pirates who terrorized villages in southern China.

In modern times, Cindy Kays has served as a pirate on the Lost Pearl, a big red pirate ship that has sailed up and down the coasts of Virginia Beach, Virginia, and Tampa, Florida.

If you were lucky enough to join a pirate adventure on the Lost Pearl, you might recall meeting Red-Eye Jack, or Bootsnatch Bill, or Irate Irene. But you probably never met Cindy Kays.

(Cindy Kays)

(Cindy Kays)

On ship, she's known as Amazing Grace. And she certainly is amazing. Her hard work and skills were quickly recognized and she soon became Lead Pirate, training others in the many skills necessary on-board ship.

She'll admit that her start as a professional pirate was a little shaky. "I got sea sick on our first voyage. I lost the battle between the heat and the rocking boat. I quickly learned to eat a little just before going out."

Being a professional pirate is not all fun and games. There's a lot of work. And just like in olden days, it starts with swabbing the deck. With a captain and four crew members, someone has to keep the ship safe and clean and that job rests with the crew.

Then there's all the fun: young visitors help pass cannon balls across the ship, load the cannon, play hot-potato with a skull, and stay low and limber with a limbo dance. The highlight of each cruise was using water cannons to attack Blackbeard's ghost who lurks around the shallow marshes.

And then there are the jokes. Love them or roll your eyes at them, it's going to be a long cruise and laughter helps pass the time.

- When they found the crocodile dead,
they knew that Captain Hook had a hand in it.

- Q: Why couldn't the pirates play cards?
A: They were standing on the deck!

- Q: Where does Captain Hook do his shopping?
A: At the second-hand store.

- Q: Why couldn't the little boy go to the pirate movie?
A: It was rated Arrrrrrrr!

- Q: What's a pirates favorite restaurant?
A: Arrrrby's!

- Q: What's a pirates second favorite restaurant?
A: Haaaaarrrrdee's!

- Q: What's a pirates third favorite restaurant?
A: Long John Silver's!

- Q: Where do pirates like to shop?
A: Taaarrrget!

- Q: How do they pay?
A: With a credit caaarrrd!

- Q: What did the ocean say to the shore?
A: Nothing. It just waved.

Fun Fact!

Gonzorgo the Pirate lifts his eye patch.

You might think that pirates wore an eye patch when someone lost an eye to a stray sword or the careless use of a giant hook. In real life, many pirates used the eye patch as a low-tech version of "Night Vision Goggles."

Imagine that you are a pirate fighting on the deck of an opponent's ship. Your goal is not just to win the fight, but to get the gold and treasures which are down below in the dark "hold" of the ship. Running below after being in the bright sunlight would be risky, especially if you've never been on the ship before. By wearing an eye patch on one eye, you can fight in the bright sunlight. When you are ready to go below, you switch the patch to the other eye which can more easily see in the dark, lower portions of the ship.

The effectiveness of this simple technique was demonstrated on the television show "MythBusters." The team proved that this practice was a great way to help improve vision in dark surroundings.

Modern night vision goggles are a lot bigger than an eye patch! (Shutterstock)

Cindy has loved performing from an early age in Pennsylvania. She wrote her first play in the sixth grade. She was a member of both the drama club and glee club in junior and senior high school. She moved to Virginia and worked in a music store, then joined with her friend

(Cindy Kays)

Shelly Potter to form the award-winning musical group C. Shells. Her pirate career began in 2007 and continued until the Lost Pearl moved from Virginia Beach to Tampa, Florida. Cindy went to Tampa to train the new crew to continue the ship's traditions of fun and safety.

So, if you'd like a life as a professional pirate, Cindy recommends that you have a good work ethic, a great sense of humor, and know how to swab the deck. It's not all glamorous, but how many jobs allow you to sing sea chanties, fire a water cannon, and get a visit from a ghost?

Water Cannon fight with Blackbeard's Ghost. (Cindy Kays)

Helpful Tips from other Character Actors

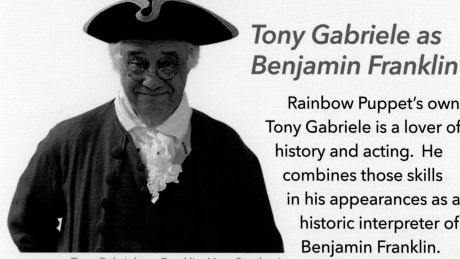

Tony Gabriele as Benjamin Franklin

Rainbow Puppet's own Tony Gabriele is a lover of history and acting. He combines those skills in his appearances as a historic interpreter of Benjamin Franklin.

Tony Gabriele as Franklin. (Ann Sanders)

He offers this insight to anyone interested in interpreting historic characters: "You want a character who has good stories to tell. Stories engage people and make history come alive. Ben Franklin has been a great character to interpret, because most people, even if they don't know much about his life, have a positive image of him. You walk into a room, and people are prepared to like him. You don't have to work hard to win them over. Still, you have to know your stuff... in detail. You have a responsibility to present a truthful picture."

Ben Franklin was amazing. In addition to helping to craft the Declaration of Independence, he invented the lightning rod, bifocal glasses, swimming fins, and the Franklin stove which revolutionized home heating. Ben Franklin created the first public library. He valued reading and once said: "An education is an investment with the greatest returns."

Nathan Richardson as Frederick Douglass

According to Nathan Richardson, the difference between an actor and a historic interpreter is found in the way they prepare. An actor prepares by learning every word in the printed script, then finding a way to bring those words to life. Usually there is a "fourth wall" which is an imaginary glass wall that allows the audience to see and hear what is going on in the play but without direct interaction between the actor and the audience. As a historic interpreter the goal is the complete removal of that wall. Nathan brings noted writer and reformer Frederick Douglass to life for modern audiences.

"If the audience interrupts, and they can, you must be prepared," says Nathan. Believe it or not, he must be most prepared for

Nathan Richardson as Frederick Douglass. (Nathan Richardson)

the questions from children who often ask very direct and personal questions such as "Did you have a dog?" "What was his name?" Nathan is well-prepared. Frederick Douglass did have a beloved dog named Frank. The giant mastiff would sit calmly as Frederick would work on his books and newspaper articles.

Nathan's transformation into Douglass is amazing. That's his real beard combined with a very well-crafted wig that turns him into the noted abolitionist.

Douglass escaped enslavement and quickly realized that his power to change others came through the ability to read and write. He was following a thought from an African fable: "Until the lion learns to read and write, history will always glorify the hunter."

It was through the power of words, in his autobiography and newspaper articles, that a nation and a president were changed. It was clear that a war to end slavery was coming. Douglass met abolitionist John Brown.

Intertwined Lives: A Statue of Lincoln & Douglass at the National Harbor in Maryland. (Shuttershock)

He admired John's willingness to take action but felt that his plans were flawed. History would prove Douglass right. By working with President Abraham Lincoln, he was able to transform America. So close was the bond between Lincoln and Douglass, that after the President's assassination, his widow gifted Douglass with a walking cane that he used the rest of his life. Nathan is the proud owner of an exact copy of that cane, which he uses in every performance.

Practically every major event in Nathan's life has combined to help him become Frederick Douglass. He was born into a family of poets who appreciated the power of language. His 22 years in the military helped him appreciate the sacrifices necessary to protect freedom. His time working for the Suffolk News-Herald helped him understand the business of sharing news... the business that Douglass used to tell his story and share his dreams. His time at Newport News Shipbuilding mirrored Frederick Douglass' time as a boat builder.

Nathan Richardson with his replica cane.
(Nathan Richardson)

Those experiences have helped create an amazing performer.

 Quotes from Frederick Douglass:

"Once you learn to read, you will be free forever."

"Liberty is meaningless where the right to utter one's thoughts and opinions has ceased to exist."

Under the Sea

Mermaids have had the world under their spell for centuries. Stories of the half human – half fish date back to ancient Assyria and spread throughout Africa, Asia, Europe, and around the world.

In many cultures, mermaids were to be avoided at all costs. Seafarers were warned that a beautiful mermaid would use her charms to lure a sailor to his death.

A gentler and more lovable mermaid appears in Hans Christian Andersen's classic story, "The Little Mermaid." A young mermaid ventures from the bottom of the ocean to the surface where she sees and falls in love with a handsome prince. The story has gained even more fans through the Disney movie and Broadway show.

Legendary explorer Christopher Columbus insisted that he saw three live mermaids while sailing near Hispaniola in 1493. He said, "They are not half as beautiful as they are painted." In reality, Columbus had spotted manatees swimming near his ship.

A manatee. (Shutterstock)

23

Woodblock of Barnum's "Fiji Mermaid." (Public Domain)

The showman and legendary huckster P. T. Barnum displayed what he insisted was a stuffed mermaid in his American Museum in New York City. According to Barnum, the mermaid was found off the Fiji Islands. In truth, the "Feejee Mermaid" was a hideous combination of a monkey and a fish. Still, thousands flocked to see the attraction. As Barnum was quoted as saying,

"There's a sucker born every minute."

So, what about "real" mermaids?

MEET MERMAID HALES

Visiting the giant aquarium at the Virginia Living Museum is usually a quiet and relaxing experience. But on this special day, the room is packed with children and their families squeezing up close to the tank. They are glad to see the loggerhead sea turtle gently moving through the water. A few of them are scared of the shark that effortlessly glides by. But the crowd is not here to see the turtle or the shark or any of the other typical creatures. They have been promised something extraordinary and that's what they will get.

Chris Mangune - (Visual Artistry Media)

Suddenly, a scuba diver jumps into the tank. He moves to the back corner. The crowd waves and the diver waves back. Still, that's not what they've come to see. Finally, there is a rustling at the top of the tank and then a huge rippling splash. As the water clears, the crowd cheers. Unbelievably, there is a breathtakingly-beautiful mermaid swimming around with the other creatures. A real mermaid! She must be. She has no air tank like the diver and the scales on her tail certainly must prove she is a living mermaid. She flips in a circle and then moves toward the front of the tank to wave at her adoring and awe-struck fans.

Mermaid Hales. (David Haycox)

It's Mermaid Hales. And no, she's not a real mermaid. But she certainly dives, swims, and looks like a real mermaid. Since her first dive into an aquarium tank, she has entertained fans at the Virginia Aquarium, the Audubon Aquarium in New Orleans, the Sea Life Aquarium in Kansas City, and many other locations.

Her real-life story is as amazing as the enchanting character she portrays. From an early age, Hales was fascinated by the ocean and sea life. She read and studied all she could find. In her studies she heard of people who would wear an elaborate costume tail and "become a mermaid." So, Hales developed strong swimming and diving skills.

It may look and sound very glamorous but there is a lot of training involved. Hales is Advanced Open Water Scuba certified and she's Free Diver Level 1 certified. Clearly, she's very comfortable in the water. But she does not use a scuba tank when appearing as a mermaid. She holds her breath and returns to the surface when she needs additional air. When floating static, she can hold her breath for up to four minutes!

She doesn't spend all of her "mermaid time" under water. With helpers, she appears at birthday parties, libraries, schools and other events to share her love of the ocean.

Hales has a theory on the popularity of mermaids. "Unlike many costume characters, we don't wear a mask. We can look at children directly and make a connection that many characters can't. It makes us very accessible. And it allows me to be very successful as an ambassador for the ocean. I can talk for the fish, and sea horses, and other creatures that live along the coast of Virginia Beach. And I can weave in a message of how important it is to protect our coast and waters."

But Hale's love of all things water doesn't end with her swimming, diving, and mermaid skills. She is a graduate of the University of Virginia with a degree in Environmental Science and a focus on Marine Science.

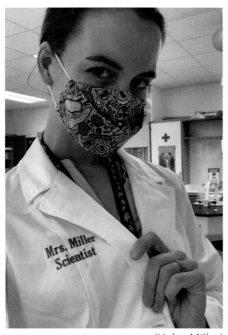
(Hales Miller)

And there's even more! She's a high school biology teacher in Hampton Roads, Virginia. Imagine having a biology teacher who is a certified scuba diver and a "real life" mermaid who has spent a significant amount of time in the water with the very creatures she talks about in class.

You might think she'd be intimidated or scared of swimming in a tank of sharks. There is a scuba diver present at all times but Hales insists that the zebra sharks are very gentle sharks. "They have little teeth. They eat clams, not people. The zebra shark stays out of my way. They are completely harmless unless they are provoked."

Her time in the aquarium tank is generally limited to 20-minute segments. "It's very cold in the water and unlike scuba divers, I am not wearing a protective wet suit."

You might also be surprised to know that when she is appearing as a mermaid, she can't really see the public on the other side of the glass. "It's almost like swimming in front of a mirror. I can see flashes from cameras or the sparkling, light-up wands that some children bring with them. Occasionally, I can see someone who comes right up to the glass."

So, what advice does Hales offer to anyone who'd like to be a mermaid:

- Practice swimming. You're going to spend a lot of time in the water.

- Make sure you have a "helper" with you at all times. Your legs are bound up in the tail so movement on land is difficult. You will need someone to help you navigate your way around.

- Learn as much as you can about the ocean and how to protect the creatures that live there. You are an ambassador for those animals.

There are job opportunities appearing at local birthday parties, aquariums across the country, and at Weeki Wachee Springs Park in Florida, where mermaids have appeared in a specially built underwater theater since 1947.

(Chris Mangune - Visual Artistry Media)

Beyond Belief!

Ask most young children today about unicorns and they might describe a cute pony-like creature with a sparkling horn on the top of their head. They might mention a creature that is shy, honest, magical, and lovable.

Unicorns are found throughout medieval European culture as a sign of purity. In ancient artwork they appear as either a goat or horse-like creature with a single horn. Their horns possess healing properties but the creatures can only be captured by a young girl who is pure of heart.

Belief in the power of the unicorn was so real and strong that dishonest vendors would sell the pointed tusks of male narwhals as unicorn horns to help people cure whatever illness they might have. This practice of selling tusks is similar to the dangers that rhinoceroses face today. Some cultures still believe that rhinoceros horns have special powers.

Ancient tapestry featuring a unicorn.
(Public Domain)

Elasmotherium, a prehistoric ancestor of the Rhinoceros.
(Painted by Heinrich Harder/Public Domain)

A prehistoric ancestor to the rhinoceros, called an Elasmotherium, looks like a more rugged version of today's unicorn. That more rugged image of a unicorn is more like the unicorns described in Hebrew mythology. This may have lead early English translators of the Bible to described a powerful creature seeking justice as a unicorn.

Even before the European unicorns, Japan adapted a Chinese mythological character into a creature very similar to a unicorn. The Kirin looks gentle and peaceful until it senses that a pure person is endangered. Then it becomes a fierce warrior.

Unicorns do not exist in Greek mythology. Ancient Greeks believed that unicorns were real creatures that existed in distant lands. Their mythology did include a similar creature. The Pegasus was a strong horse-like creature with giant wings that would allow it to fly across the sky.

In the story, the Pegasus was the child of Medusa, a female with venomous snakes, instead of hair, coming out from her head. One look at Medusa would turn a person to stone. She was eventually destroyed by the hero Perseus who took her winged baby Pegasus and flew off on its back to find other adventures.

A Pegasus helps Douglas Fairbanks fly in this movie poster. (Public Domain)

Medusa was the mother of the Pegasus. (Shutterstock)

While these early accounts of the Pegasus and the unicorn describe creatures who can be quite fierce when necessary, it still might be exciting to ride one.

MEET TATIANA AND KANAT

If there's one thing you can count on at a huge arena circus, it's the roar of the crowd. The cheering, the clapping, the discussion of what's going to happen next all blend together into a noise that is addictive to circus performers.

That's why Tatiana Tchalabaeva was so startled the first time she rode her Pegasus into a huge arena. All the lights dimmed, the music played softly, and as she rode her creature around the giant hall she was stunned by the absolute silence.

Tatiana Tchalabaeva riding Pegasus. (Kanat Riders)

Normally, that kind of silence would mean that the audience had walked out or they had never shown up in the first place. Either would be devastating to a performer. But that's not what was happening. The audience was literally in awe of what they were seeing… a beautiful Queen on her radiant winged Pegasus being greeted by her handsome King, riding a unicorn.

This event happened not once, but at performance after performance, night after night for two full years.

Before she rode that magical creature, Tatiana Tchalabaeva was born in Kazakhtsan, which borders Russia and China. It was there that she met her husband, Kanat. She was a National Team Gymnast. He was part of a famous Cossack Riding Act.

Riding and difficult acrobatic stunts were a family tradition for Kanat. His father was a gymnast, his mother was part of the Cossack Riding act.

The act is fast-paced and thrilling as riders stand atop galloping horses. They create moving human pyramids atop two horses running side by side. They hop off of their saddles and flip completely under the horse and then back on top again as the horses run at breakneck speed.

Husband and wife onstage. (Kanat Riders)

Tatiana and Kanat came to America as part of a Mongolian-themed edition of Ringling Brothers and Barnum & Bailey Circus. Kanat eventually created his own act and became the trainer of new riders with even more impressive skills. Tatiana became a part of that riding act, combining her sense of style, beauty, and presentation. But don't think she's there just for show. As her horse gallops madly around the track, she leans off of her saddle, her head inches from the floor, and fearlessly grabs scarves from the center of the ring.

Now married, and with two daughters, the family appeared in other editions of the Ringling show. They also appeared with UniverSoul Circus. Tatiana thought she'd end up in New York teaching gymnastics, instead, the family was called by Cirque du Soleil. While waiting to perform with that circus in Canada they got another request from

Tatiana Tchalabaeva onstage. (Kanat Riders)

Kanat Tchalabaeva onstage. (Kanat Riders)

Ringling Brothers. Would the family return with their riding act, and could they add a unicorn and a Pegasus?

Add a unicorn and a Pegasus? Okay.

The unicorn was created by a special headpiece on the bridle of the horse. No problem at all.

The Pegasus was created by wings attached to the horse's saddle. The framework was made of metal and was perfectly balanced. Practice sessions helped the horse get used to the feel of the wings and learn to move with ease.

The results were magical. And while most of the audience was awestruck and silent, one little voice could be heard from the audience every night. Tatiana's youngest daughter Veranica pointing and screaming proudly, "That's my mamma! That's my mamma!"

Just as Kanat learned skills from his mother and father, those skill are being passed on to the next generation. Veranica is now in 6th grade and is learning all sorts of circus acts. She can bravely stand atop two side by side horses, one foot on each saddle. She's learned to work on the

trapeze and learned to walk on the challenging "Wheel of Death." She currently performs a terrific poodle act with the family shows.

Her older sister Angelica also performs as needed but Tatiana is most proud that her daughter is working to become an anesthesiologist. She assists a local oral surgeon and is in

Veranica on horses. (Tatiana Tchalabaeva)

college, receiving scholarships, producing constant appearances on the Dean's list, and achieving perfect grades.

So, what advice does Tatiana offer to anyone wanting to ride a magical unicorn or Pegasus?

Angelica onstage. (Tatiana Tchalabaeva)

"Riding the Pegasus is the easiest riding I've ever done in a show. You go around the track and people are thrilled. What's hard is everything that leads up to it. Learning to ride, up in the early morning to care for the horses, making sure the costumes are set out and ready, checking on the horses again, constant travel from town to town, working with the horses again. It's all very hard work. But I love it. And if you can do what you love with the people you love, that is truly magical."

The Tchalabaeva family: Angelica, Kanat, Veranica and Tatiana. (Tatiana Tchalabaeva)

Touch a Rainbow

Rainbows are amazing. Even after a terrible storm, we are often greeted with those bright and beautiful ribbons of light wrapping across the sky.

In Bible times, the Rainbow sealed a promise God made to Noah. He would never again send a flood to destroy the entire world.

In "The Wizard of Oz," Dorothy dreams of leaving the drab, colorless plains of Kansas. She hopes to travel "Over the Rainbow" to an enchanted land filled with joy and color.

In "The Muppet Movie," Kermit the Frog plays his banjo and sings of his wish to find the secrets that lie on the other side of a rainbow.

In Ireland, it is believed that you'll meet a Leprechaun and find a glowing pot of gold at the end of a rainbow.

The trouble is, it's impossible to actually reach the end of the rainbow. Rainbows are formed by sunlight hitting droplets of water or fog. It is refracted or split into different colors. The colors spread out from red to violet. Some people use the name "Roy G. Biv" to remember the order of the colors: Red, Orange, Yellow, Green, Blue, Indigo, Violet.

While the promise of the rainbow is comforting and many people dream of traveling either over, to the other side, or to the end of a rainbow, there is one group of people that get

Laura Baldwin making repairs to the Rainbow.

to see and touch a rainbow hundreds of times a year. The Rainbow Puppeteers set up a rainbow backstage for almost every show.

This Rainbow was lovingly created by Helen Spaetzel, an artist who built many puppets, painted many sets, and sewed the Rainbow the team has used for over 25 years. It is a good memory of her that is especially appreciated by her student, fellow puppeteer, and puppet maker, Laura Baldwin. For Laura, Helen's work with Rainbow Puppets opened the door to years of making extraordinary puppet creations.

MEET LAURA BALDWIN

Rainbow Puppeteer Wesley Huff loves to tell the story of how his mother walked into their home carrying a giant broken beach umbrella she had found in a pile of rubbish on the side of the road. She exclaimed, "I'll bet I can turn this umbrella into a puppet."

Wesley said, "Mom, can you go anywhere without seeing something that can be turned into a puppet?" As Wesley has now learned, the answer to that question is "no."

Laura Baldwin has a unique gift that allows her to see how discarded items can be transformed into fabulous puppets. In the case of the beach umbrella, she combined it with the fabric from a thrift store evening gown and created a startling, giant spider puppet for Rainbow's production of TOYLAND.

Giant spider puppet. (Rainbow Puppets)

It doesn't stop with the beach umbrella. When she was making the chicken puppet for the show NOAH'S FLOATING ZOO, she wanted the puppet to have feathers that would remain colorful and thick though many, many performances.

Laura Baldwin with Hennie the Hen. Those feathers are actually silk flower petals.

Real feathers would fall apart after a few shows. She tried one thing after another. In desperation, she prayed about her problem. Immediately, the answer came to her – she could unravel the petals of silk flowers and then use them as feathers on the puppet. They were beautiful, colorful, and remain so in performances 25 years after the puppet was first made.

Vacuum cleaner hoses, pool noodles, giant plastic Easter eggs, clothes hangers, and so much more have found their way into Laura's creations.

The realistic eyes of the wooly mammoth puppet in THE REALLY BIG DINOSAUR SHOW were made from the plastic cases used to hold toys in vending machines. She painted the inside of the clear shells dark brown. The plastic gives the eyes a natural, life-like shine. By the way, the hair on the top of the mammoth's head is really the yarn from an old floor mop.

Wesley Huff demonstrates how the mouth of the Great White Egret Puppet is working for his mother, puppet maker Laura Baldwin.

Laura (right) with her mentor and friend, Helen Spaetzel. In addition to making puppets, the two crafted a celebrated collection of Santa images called "The Baltzel Belsnichols." (They combined their last names to create "Baltzel.") (Laura Baldwin)

Laura credits good friend and mentor Helen Spaetzel for helping her learn to build puppets. She's not shy about asking for help. When building a puppet version of Patrick Henry, she got advice from a wig maker at

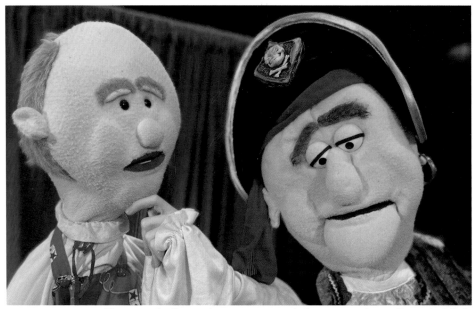

The gentle Toymaker puppet and the scary pirate Captain Mick.

Colonial Williamsburg. When searching for life-like eyes for her Abraham Lincoln puppet, she tracked down a gifted artist in New York City who sent her the needed parts. The final puppet is impressive, always getting gasps from audience members when he walks on stage.

Laura with a mamma and baby maiasaura. Part of "The Really Big Dinosaur Show."

She's also willing to try again and again until she gets the puppet just right. It took two attempts to get her Megazostrodon puppet the right size. It also took two attempts to get the Toymaker's face to look warm and gentle.

The first version had a crooked nose and looked a bit scary. That all worked out for the best as the scary version was later turned into the evil pirate Captain Mick for the show PIRATE PARTY.

So, if you'd like to be like Laura, and touch rainbows and create amazing puppets here are some tips:

- Ask questions. Anyone you meet might be able to help you learn new skills. Laura once needed help tying a knot to securely hold a marionette (string) puppet together. She saw that someone near her house had a boat so she figured they liked to fish and would know some strong knots. She knocked on their door and was soon treated to a class in knot tying!

- Remember the 12-foot rule. This is something she learned from her mentor, Helen Spaetzel, but it's an old theater saying. Don't just look at your puppet up close. Move back 12-feet and see what it looks like from there. That's where your audience will be viewing your work and it may look different from there.

- Don't give up. Not every attempt will work. Laura sometimes has to build more than one version of a puppet or puppet part until she gets it perfect.

Scary Sights!

According to the National Retail Federation, Americans spent 8.05 billion dollars on Halloween in 2020. And that's a number that has been growing year after year. Only a fourth of that money is spent on candy. The majority is spent on costumes and elaborate decorations. Most of them scary. People like to be scared.

One way to get a good scare is to visit the ghost tours found in historic towns across the country. All promise a scary good time. Some insist that they are regularly startled by unexpected visits and occurrences. While you might be brave enough to seek out an occasional scare, do you have what it takes to seek out spooks night after night after night?

(Ghost Tours of Harpers Ferry)

MEET RICK GARLAND

In the daylight Harpers Ferry, West Virginia, is a quaint little town overlooking a spot where two rivers and three states converge. When the sun goes down, it's a very different place. The joyful muffled sounds from the little shops and restaurants give way to an unsettling silence that seems to warn that something dreadful is about to happen. It's as if all of the tragedy and horrors that have fallen upon this unique location are ready to bubble up and terrify you at any moment. And that moment gets a little help from Mr. Rick Garland.

Rick Garland. (Ghost Tours of Harpers Ferry)

Garland is the tour guide and operator of "Ghost Tours of Harpers Ferry." It is the oldest such tour in the country and one of the most highly rated. Trip Advisor guests recently voted it the best ghost tour in the nation.

Harpers Ferry. (Shutterstock)

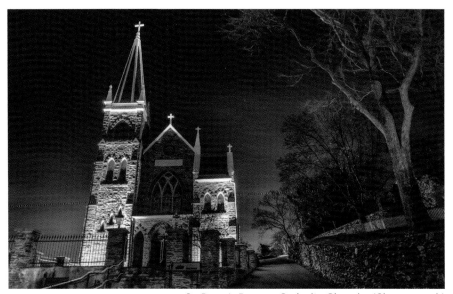
St. Peter's Roman Catholic Church. (Shutterstock)

He starts his tours on the steps outside of St. Peter's Roman Catholic Church at the highest point of the city. Because of his religious beliefs, he makes it clear that neither he nor the tour is involved in any paranormal activities that would attempt to conjure any spirits. He is a history enthusiast who tells scary stories associated with the town of Harpers Ferry.

And he does a wonderful job setting the stage for a night full of scary stories. As the sun sets, he discusses the importance of the Potomac and Shenandoah rivers and the states of Virginia, West Virginia, and Delaware which created the opportunities and heartache that fell on Harpers Ferry.

The city was a flashpoint during the Civil War as John Brown led an unsuccessful raid to try to free enslaved African Americans. Throughout the war, the North and South fought for access to its gun manufacturing plant. Between fires and skirmishes the city changed from Union to Confederate 8 to 12 times, depending on who's counting.

A whistle blows eerily as a train makes its way across the high bridge into the tunnel carved into the nearby mountain wall. Above the entrance to the tunnel is a stone marker noting the tunnel's construction date... 1931. Is it fate? That's the year Universal Studios unleashed Dracula and Frankenstein on the world. Now, by the light of an oil lantern, Rick unleashes a stream of terrifying tales.

He seamlessly mixes historical facts with tales of dishes violently flying across a restaurant and unexplained sounds at the top of a stairway. A stop on a side street brings the tale of hungry pigs, a violent death, and an innocent victim that still cries out for mercy and revenge.

I promised Rick I would not tell any of the stories from his tour in this book. Instead, I will share the story and the scary experience he does NOT tell on his tours. It's the event that still leaves him quite shaken when he thinks about it.

Harpers Ferry was owned, in large part by Mr. Harper. He amassed a huge fortune in gold during his lifetime and told no one where he hid it except his wife Rachel. For years after his death in 1862, Rachel would search for the gold in the garden and root cellar but to no avail. At night it was rumored she would stare out her window into the garden below to make sure no one tried to steal the gold.

Rick stands with his back to that very window when he tells some of the scariest stories of the evening. He does not tell the story of Mrs. Harper staring out the window feeling it is not the strongest of tales. But one night, after a tour, a woman claiming to be a physic came up to Rick and asked about the woman in the window behind him staring down to the ground below. A woman, staring out of Mrs. Harper's window?

More unsettling, a week later, another woman claiming to be a psychic said she saw that same woman staring down to the crowd below. Was it Mrs. Harper still guarding her husband's gold? Or just a chance coincidence? But still, the house has been unoccupied for decades so it really couldn't be anyone. Could it?

Shirley Doughtery, creator of the tour.
(Ghost Tours of Harpers Ferry)

Most of the stories in the tour were collected and told by Harpers Ferry resident, restaurant owner and unofficial historian Shirley Dougherty. She collected many of the stories into the book "A Ghostly Tour of Harpers Ferry" and would lead nightly tours.

When she was unable to continue the work, her granddaughter took over. Her granddaughter did the tour until one night, when she returned from a tour shaken and confused. To this day, she's told no one what she saw or heard... she only exclaimed that she would never give another ghost tour again.

At this same time, Rick was in Gettysburg, Pennsylvania, considering his career options. He had gone from injured college basketball player to working at a hotel, to filling out tax forms, to landscaping, to finally singing historic songs at night with a friend who was a former Broadway actor. While business was good for quite a while, eventually his friend returned to Broadway and Gettysburg became flooded with 24 nightly ghost tour companies. With so many nightly entertainment options, it was clear that his nights of singing historic songs were coming to an end.

Fortunately, his wife's grandmother heard of the potential to run the ghost tours in Harpers Ferry and declared, "If you don't do this... somebody else will." Telling stories and sharing history in Harpers Ferry? Rick jumped at the chance. And it's been an exciting adventure. He's carefully crafted the tour into a nightly adventure that entertains, educates, and offers some scares along the way.

Are you thinking of following his footsteps as a teller of terror? Here is some advice he offers:

- "Learn something from every job you do. From my years working with hotels, I learned to spot potential problem guests and made them at ease the moment they walked in the door. I use that now to steer my presentations."

- "Be well-read. In the history business, it is important to learn as much as you can. And keep learning all the time."

- "Don't make up facts. If you don't know, say you don't know. It's better to not know than to share something that's not right."

- "Connect with the children in the group. If you keep them entertained and happy, their parents and the other adults in the crowd will usually follow along in having fun."

And what could be more fun than having your wits scared by Rick Garland on the "Ghost Tour of Harpers Ferry?"

WHAT CAN IT BE?

(Ghost Tours of
Harpers Ferry)

Rick's wife Amelia also conducts tours. Some people insist there is an unfortunate prisoner walking behind her.

A tour participant posted this. What is that image seen on the upper level of this house?

(Ghost Tours of Harpers Ferry)

Meet the Monsters!

In 1981, ex-construction worker Bob Chandler drove his modified, giant wheeled truck he called Bigfoot over a collection of junk cars. He did it as a joke to show off his work. The joke has turned into a motor sport phenomenon that seems to become more popular with every passing year.

Arenas, fairs, and beaches across the country feature the rumbling, noisy machines. Visitors can stop by the legendary Grave Digger's Dungeon on their way to the Outer Banks. At the Dungeon, you can learn the history of one of the sport's iconic trucks. If you're brave enough, you can ride in a Monster Truck before you leave.

But what would it be like to build and operate a monster truck for a living?

Moster Trucks have become a popular motor sport. (Pixabay)

MEET DONNY HEBERT

By the age of 13, Donny Hebert had saved up his money and bought his first mud truck. Working with his dad, he broke and fixed that truck over and over. Along the way, he was developing the skills he now uses to maintain and operate monster trucks.

Donny was willing to take all sorts of jobs to get the money to get into the Monster Truck business, but there was one job he wouldn't do. "I wouldn't work as an auto mechanic. I don't have the patience to work on other people's vehicles, yet I'll spend all night and day working on my own."

Donny and Aftershock. (Donny Hebert)

And there's a lot of work to keep his trucks running. "We're taking 12,000-pound machines and sending them 30 feet into the air. Nothing was designed to do that. We're doing things that engineers wouldn't dream of a few years back. Now, we do it several times a day every single weekend," says Donny.

(Monster Truckz)

Donny says this tire may look bad, but you should see the RV he drove over. (Donny Hebert)

Today, he is the owner and driver of AfterShock and Tyrone the Terrible. He also serves as Talent Coordinator for Monster Truckz, a company that presents shows across the county. He contracts drivers and trucks for the two editions that are on the road. In that role, he has seen what it takes to be successful in the business.

"First, and foremost, this is a business. And it's a very demanding business," he says. "We work 15 to 20 hours a day, setting up, making repairs, performing, and then more repairs and maintenance. If something breaks, you've got to fix it. There's no taking it to a shop and hoping they have the

(Donny Hebert)

skills and parts to make the repairs. Then there's the travel, from location to location. We live on the road."

While it is a business, Donny wouldn't consider doing anything else. The sound of the engines, the cheers of the crowd, and seeing his machines do the impossible make it all worthwhile.

And his advice to anyone wishing to become part of the business?

- "Find a local team. Visit them, tell them you want to help. Then prove your worth."

- "This is a job. It's not standing around taking pictures and posting them all day long."

- "Love what you're doing. It's going to take up a lot of your time."

Imagine going to school like this? (Monster Truckz)

*Here is 11-year old Hunter, son of Monster Truckz owner Zach Garden.
It looks like he's ready to join the team.* (Monster Truckz)

To the Moon and Beyond!

Before recorded history began, it is believed that humans would look up into the sky and dream of what could be. At some point, they imagined that the stars outlined shapes which often resembled the characters in their myths and legends.

The mysteries of the heavens opened up further with the use of telescopes. Now, the moon, the stars and planets became closer than ever before. At some point, it was not enough to just look into the sky... people dreamed of actually traveling to the moon and beyond.

In May of 1961, John F. Kennedy said "I believe that this Nation should commit itself to achieving the goal, before this decade is out, of landing a man on the Moon and returning him safely to Earth." We met that challenge and continue to find ways to explore what lies beyond our planet.

Apollo 11 moon landing. (NASA)

So, what would it be like to see what lies beyond our planet, and beyond our universe?

MEET JODY DAVIS

Some people struggle their entire life to find what they truly love and where they excel. Other people seem to find their passion right away. As a little girl in Minnesota, Jody Davis loved gazing into the sky and dreaming of what might be. She loved what she saw but wanted to see so much more. By the time she was eight years old, her parents bought her a red telescope.

Jody Davis. (NASA)

She would go out into a dark field with them to gaze at the stars and planets above... dreaming of what might be... and hoping to go further than ever before.

To say that Jody is focused and motivated would be an understatement. She was flying an airplane solo before she could legally get her learner's permit to drive a car. She worked at a beauty salon after school where she earned money to pay for the flight lessons. At the age of 13, she saw the movie "Apollo 13." A NASA mission with three astronauts headed to the moon turns into a fight for survival as their systems start to fail. Engineers back on the ground must quickly come together and find a way to repair the spacecraft and get them safely home. The film and mission cemented Jody's plan to become an engineer.

She received a Bachelor of Science degree in aerospace engineering from Embry-Riddle Aeronautical University and a Master of Science degree in mechanical and aerospace engineering from the University of Virginia. Her master's degree research included time at NASA's Langley Research Center in Hampton, Virginia. She's been at NASA ever since.

Her team was responsible for getting the Curiosity Mars Rover safely onto the red planet. The data this car-sized rover collects has helped us understand that the Martian environment used to once be a habitable place.

As exciting as her work on the Mars project was, Jody still wanted more. Going back to her first experience gazing through a telescope, she jumped at the chance to work with other engineers to

Curiosity Mars Rover. (NASA)

design and build two of the most powerful telescopes to be launched into space.

Jody was responsible for helping build the James Webb Space Telescope, launched in December of 2021. It is the largest space telescope ever launched, about the size of

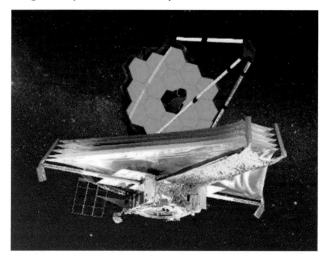

a tennis court, in an orbit 1 million miles from Earth. "It will allow us to see things we haven't even imagined." Jody adds, "We

The Webb Telescope. (NASA)

The Webb Telescope. (NASA)

will be able to see and study light from the first stars and galaxies formed just after the Big Bang."

Jody is now responsible for helping coordinate the design and assembly of the Nancy Grace Roman Space Telescope, planned for launch in 2026. The Roman Telescope is about the size of the Hubble Space Telescope which is currently the most powerful. Roman will have a field of view 100 times greater than Hubble. Roman will help us understand the expansion of our universe and explore extrasolar planets within our galaxy. Extrasolar planets are objects that may be rotating around stars other than our sun.

Helping us land a rover on Mars, unlocking secrets of the universe unseen for billions of years. That would be enough for one lifetime, right? No. In her "spare time," Jody has set a goal to run a marathon on every continent on the globe.

Artist Illustration of the Roman Telescope. (NASA)

In 2018, she climbed to the top of Mount Kilimanjaro in Tanzania. From the highest spot of the African continent, she still wasn't done. She returned to the country, providing telescopes and teaching STEM classes to young women who might gaze into the skies and lead the next wave of space exploration.

Jody and her class in Tanzania. (Jody Davis)

MEET ALVIN DREW

Helping others in their quest for knowledge is part of the NASA culture. Astronaut Alvin Drew certainly demonstrates that mind-set. It's not unusual to find him in a school room answering questions from students or meeting with children and their families at events like Pioneer Days at the Smithsonian National Air and Space Museum in Chantilly, Virginia.

As a four-year-old, Alvin wanted to be a pilot. By the time Apollo 11 landed on the moon, he then wanted to be an astronaut at age six. Through hard work, he achieved both goals. Through hard work, he achieved both goals.

Alvin Drew's official portrait. (NASA)

As a decorated Air Force Pilot, he flew combat missions in Desert Shield, Desert Storm, and many other operations. He was then selected to be an astronaut and twice flew on the Space Shuttle to the International Space Station.

In an online NASA interview with students, he was asked what it was like to be in space. "On earth you are hauling your weight around. In space all you are hauling around is your mass. So, you don't need your big muscles, like your quadriceps and biceps to move around. You use your finger tips and your toes to get yourself around gracefully. And for the first few days when you are pushing off with your big muscles you take off too quickly and you knock things off the wall and people recognize that you're a rookie."

When asked about food in space, he says unlike the old days, you can eat practically anything now. "Spaghetti… Steak… Cajun food… The only things we try to avoid are thing that are crumbly like popcorn or crackers because once you bite into them the crumbs don't just fall on the floor. They float around and get in people's eyes and hair and people get annoyed."

While being interviewed by Student Reporter Jaden Jefferson, he said, "I watched the Apollo 11 crew land and I asked should I become an astronaut? The next question that came out of my mouth was can somebody black actually be an astronaut.? This was just after the Civil Rights Act passed and segregation had not departed from our society. My dad said, the Air Force has already picked a black astronaut… It was all I needed to know. Once that barrier was down it was all on me at that point.

Alvin Drew on a space walk. (NASA)

If I didn't succeed it was because I had failed; not because there was some social barrier out there between me and that goal."

He quickly quotes the legendary Tuskegee Airmen leader, Major General Benjamin O. Davis, who said, "His least favorite words in the English language were 'first' and 'only.' None of the things I did were first or only... Now, it's nothing unusual. All you have to do is have the drive and work hard. And go out there and get it. There is no excuse for anyone to go out there and not try... We've been in the White House. We've been in space. What's holding you back?"

And Drew has put his time and effort behind his words, becoming the co-founder of the Patti Grace Smith Fellowship which helps others reach their goals.

Alvin Drew with the Rainbow Puppets at National Air and Space Pioneer Days.

See You Later, Alligator

In the 1950's, Rock and Roll Legend Bill Haley had a huge hit with the song "See You Later, Alligator." The song created a catch phrase that is still used today. It also offers the very good advice to stay as far away from alligators as possible.

That advice has not hindered the success of places like Gatorland in Orlando. Since 1949, the attraction has drawn fans who want to get as close as safely possible to alligators and crocodiles. Braver visitors can even zipline over marshes filled with these giant-jawed critters.

Of course, it's one thing to see these creatures on the other side of a fence. But what would it be like to be face to face with one of these monsters?

(Pixabay)

MEET TAHAR DOUIS

You would think that being listed in the Guinness Book of World Records for supporting the Heaviest Human Pyramid in History would be enough of a challenge for any performer. But not for Tahar Douis.

The Moroccan strong man held his 12-member acrobatic team on his shoulders. This was a pyramid of people three levels high, weighing 1,700 pounds!

After facing this challenge, Tahar was ready for more. It may be hard to imagine, but in the late 1970's many people across America had only seen alligators or crocodiles on television or in the movies. Because of his strength, Tahar was asked to present these unusual creatures in arenas across the country and he said, "yes."

If you're looking for Tahar Douis, you can see his feet. He is supporting the rest of his troupe. (Promotional photo, Field Entertainment)

There was a catch. As the strong man in his acrobatic troupe and now with his listing in the Guinness Book of World Records, he couldn't leave his team stranded. So Tahar would travel and perform with his troupe Friday through Sunday and then fly to Gainesville, Florida, every Monday to learn how to safely manage and work with alligators.

Tahar's trainer was Bob Tiger, a third-generation Seminole alligator handler from Florida. Years ago, Florida Seminole Native American tribe refused to sign a treaty with the United States. Instead, they moved deeper and deeper into the dangerous Everglades to remain independent. There, they learned the skills of "wrestling" and hunting alligators to survive.

Tahar underwent a full year of training. The first month was spent just watching the alligators from a distance. Then he moved in closer and the training became more intense. "These are wild creatures and will always be wild. They do not learn tricks like a horse or a lion." Tahar explains that they do exhibit behaviors. If you hold your hand above their snout they will open their mouth. "Their jaws are not strong when they open. They are very strong when they close and if they start to roll, you must let go."

(Shutterstock)

Tahar learned his lessons and after a year, Bob said, "I have nothing more to show him. He's ready." And with that, Tahar began his new career presenting alligators across America.

Tahar in action. (Wikipedia Commons/Cornstalker)

Not one to take the easy way out, Tahar worked with a wide variety of wild alligators. If an alligator became lazy or uninterested, Tahar would find another. And he confronted many in his career, including an eight foot long, hissing gator called Jumpy.

"When I am presenting alligators, I am thinking two things. First, I am thinking of the audience. How do I make this show even better than the last? Then I think of the alligators. Which one will put on a good show? Which one seems dangerous today? There is always the chance of danger."

That's a lesson that another gator presenter discovered in Norfolk, Virginia. In the middle of a performance, he was bitten by an especially mean alligator. In the tradition of "the show must go on," Tahar was flown in to continue the week of performances. Unfortunately, Tahar was attacked by the same gator! Tahar was rushed to the hospital but returned to finish out the week. After some recovery time, he was able to present his program at Madison Square Garden in New York city later that same year.

So, are you interested in facing a wild gator? If so, here's Tahar's advice: "Don't!"

He elaborates, "I last performed with alligators five years ago. I'm a very lucky man. I only had two accidents, the one in Norfolk and then later at the Mississippi State Fair. I still have a scar on my chin to prove it."

These days, he works at a posh retirement community in the Washington, D.C. area. So far, the retirees have been much nicer than the alligators.

Tahar with Olivia Newton John.
(Douis)

James Cooper and David Messick in a number that was written to pay tribute to Tahar's amazing work. Note that James and David are in less danger here than Tahar ever was.

Catch a Dinosaur!

Scientists will tell you that there were millions of years between the age of dinosaurs and the first appearance of humans. That hasn't stopped movie makers from combining people and dinosaurs in many different ways. The blockbuster film "Jurassic Park" was the beginning of a long-running film series that started in 1993 and seems to have no end in sight.

Today, people want to do more than see these creatures on the big screen. They flock to amusement parks, museums, and giant arenas to take pictures, see the creatures up close, and maybe even ride a dinosaur.

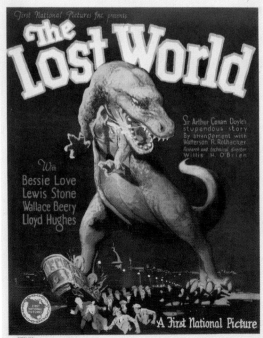

Dinosaurs and people have been combined onscreen since the early days of movies. That's "Gertie the Dinosaur" from 1914 and "The Lost World" from 1925. (Public domain)

MEET MARK CLINE

As a boy, Mark Cline remembers seeing a film called "The Valley of Gwangi." In the movie, dinosaurs are discovered in the "Forbidden Valley." A group of cowboys hope to capture a dinosaur and take it on tour for the world to see. The image of cowboys trying to lasso and ride a dinosaur was one that Mark Cline couldn't forget and one that he'd one day create for himself.

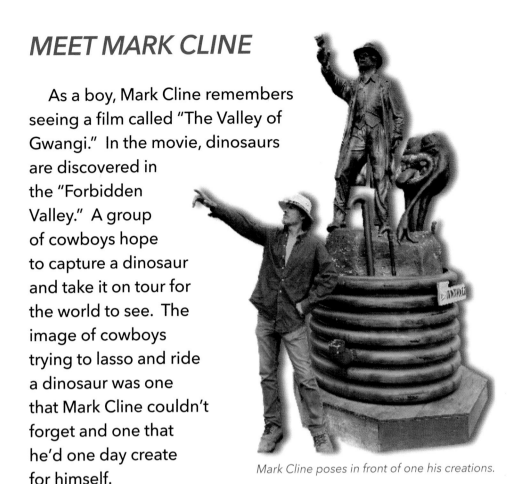

Mark Cline poses in front of one his creations.

He and his father visited "Dinosaur Land" in White Post, Virginia. As they peered through the fence into the classic roadside attraction, they saw the giant dinosaurs created by Chicago sculptor James Q. Sidwell. Mark said, "That's what I want to do." His father told him he could, if that's what he set his mind to do.

Born in Waynesboro, Virginia, Mark struggled with "book learning" but excelled in visual arts. His fourth-grade teacher Sallie Berry Spiller saw Cline's gifts and gave him the time and space in school to develop and grow his paper-mâché

sculpting skills. She saw his skills before he did.

As a teenager, working with a friend, he created paper-mâché dinosaurs that would line the river cutting through town. Later, he expanded the idea to having the audience sit as his dinosaur floated down the river on homemade boats.

Sculptures created by Cline in his "Dinosaur Kingdom II" park echo a scene from the movie "Forbidden Valley."

These first attempts at dinosaur making taught him important business lessons. First, you shouldn't put your giant dinosaurs on other people's property and hope to make money. Second, hitting rocks in the middle of the river can give your dinosaurs an unexpected tumble. Third, water is the enemy of paper-mâché. Your hard work can quickly disintegrate into a gooey mess.

After high school, a chance ride into town got him to an employment agency at the very moment Redmill Manufacturing called looking for a new worker. Not knowing what the job was, Mark said, "Whatever it is, I'll take it!"

Well, the job was making items out of resins and fiberglass. It didn't take the owner long to see that Mark was a natural.

81

A huge skull prop created by Cline for rock legend Alice Cooper.

He gave Mark a five-gallon bucket of resin to take home. "See what you can make out of this, kid!" What Mark Cline made was a career.

Soon he was creating giant statues for businesses to put beside their road signs. He created astronauts, rocket ships, and a towering mechanic holding a car muffler. For rock legend Alice Cooper, he created a huge skull prop. For a billionaire, he created a gigantic woman who appeared to be resting in a lake. As an April Fool's prank, he created a

Cline in front of his Foamhenge creation.

replica of Stonehenge that he called Foamhenge. He's built creatures for theme parks and haunted houses including the one on the boardwalk in Virginia Beach. Those giant creatures at the mini-golf course? He's made many of them as well. But most of all, he created dinosaurs! Lots and lots of dinosaurs. Best of all, his new fiberglass inventions didn't dissolve in the rain!

Two of many giant creatures built by Cline for theme parks, mini-golf courses, haunted houses and other businesses.

This sign, created by Cline, greets visitors to the "Dinosaur Kingdom II" park in Natural Bridge, Virginia.

But Mark had even bigger dreams. He wanted a dinosaur park of his own. And he still couldn't shake the image of cowboys riding dinosaurs. That image morphed into his own park called "Dinosaur Kingdom" built next to his Professor Cline's Haunted Monster Museum in Natural Bridge, Virginia.

Undeterred when a fire destroyed the museum, he was able to rebuild a bigger and better attraction across the street from the Natural Bridge Zoo. "Dinosaur Kingdom II" is a fantasy world where dinosaurs are somehow merged with soldiers during the Civil War... and all the insanity that follows when humans try to tame the giant creatures. Along the way, Bigfoot enters the picture and visitors must use water cannons to protect themselves.

We follow the trail and are startled to see Abraham Lincoln

Cline showing off his original designs for the park. Note his "Ghost Story" alter-ego behind his back.

standing on top of a house. It's Mark Cline's explanation as to why Lincoln's Gettysburg Address was so short. In Cline's world, it seems that a pterodactyl stole half of the speech.

As with all of Cline's creations, he begins with a blank piece of paper. Those sketches allow him to work with his team to create his fantasy world.

Cline offers some words of advice he's picked up along the way:

- Get your ideas down on paper. Let people see what you're thinking and creating in your head.

- Make sure your work pleases you. These are your ideas. These are your thoughts. Don't create things based on what you think others might like.

- Be thankful for teachers. I was so lucky to have a teacher who believed in me and helped me when I struggled in school.

An early newspaper image of Cline. He's still at the drawing board today, just finishing his latest illustrated book.

A triceratops is back in the shop getting a "nose job".

"Professor" Cline as he is now known, continues to create giant creatures, props, comic books, and live performances across the country. His work has been featured in art museums and on the pages of the New York Times. And from time to time, you might catch him riding on the top of one of his amazing dinosaur creations.

Mark riding an earlier Triceratops he built for Luray Caverns in the 1980's.

Final Thoughts...

Well, you've reached the end of this book. And just like the end of most of our shows, this is the time I come out and say, "So, what have we learned today?" Here's what I've learned:

Ben Cherry, the pirate guy, reminds us to enjoy what you do!

Cindy Kays, the lead pirate, reminds us that even super terrific jobs have times when you just have to, "Swab the deck!" She loved her time on the pirate ship, despite the yucky parts of the job.

Hales Miller, the mermaid, shows that it takes training in many areas to achieve some goals.

Tatiana Tchalabaeva, the Pegasus rider, reminds us to love what we do and do it with the people we love.

Laura Baldwin, the puppet maker, reminds us to ask questions. You may never learn something new if you don't ask for help.

Rick Davis, the storyteller, reminds us that we should learn something in every job we do, it will help us when we get to the next job.

Donnie Hebert reminds us that even dream jobs often require long hours and hard work.

Jody Davis, the engineer, reminds us that we have a responsibility to others... as we are working on our dreams, help others learn, grow, and achieve their dreams.

Alvin Drew, the astronaut, reminds us that our own hard work and effort are what help us achieve success. Don't wait for others to bring opportunities to you.

Tahar Douis, the "alligator guy," reminds us to be safe. Sometimes it's better to dream from afar!

Mark Cline, the dinosaur man, tells us to put our ideas on paper, so that we can let others see our dreams and help us make them a reality.

So, as you continue your journey, deciding what you enjoy doing and how to get there, I hope you'll think of these amazing people and their advice. Thank you for reading this book and joining me in my dream job.

Acknowledgments

My sincere thanks to all of the people who participated in the creation of this book. They each were gracious with their time and patience.

Ben Cherry in real life is no evil Blackbeard the Pirate. He's a gentleman who spends his time away from his evil character, with his wife Dee Gee.

Mark Cline was so generous with his time, giving our team an exclusive tour of his workshop and later, a private tour of Dinosaur Kingdom II. It's well worth the trip and while you're there, go across the street to Natural Bridge Zoo. It's a unexpectedly large park filled with amazing creatures.

I first met Jody Davis in church and only learned of her incredible career by piecing together her posts on Facebook. I'd see pictures of her at the Smithsonian National Air and Space Museum days after we visited. Of course, we were there performing but she was there getting awards for helping us get to Mars!

Tahar Douis was a childhood hero. We even perform a song with a singing caiman and toucan puppet in recognition of his skills. Of course, we are a lot less likely to get hurt.

Alvin Drew was certainly a much sought-after man the day we joined him at the Smithsonian Pioneer Days. Fortunately, we had time to speak at lunch and get a few pictures in during the day. It was an honor to be able to meet him.

Rick Garland has fans with all of the Rainbow Puppet team. We took his tour one time and were enchanted. A few years later, we were on tour and wondered how we would spend the rest of the evening. Each looked sheepishly at the other until one of us finally said, "Can we do the Ghost Tour again?" Shouts of agreement followed and we now visit whenever we are remotely close to the West Virginia area.

My thanks to Donny Hebert and Zach Garden for helping us tell about Monster Truckz. Their great success is proof that hard work pays off.

We've worked with Cindy Kays for decades now. We have been on the same bill at festivals, museums, and special events too many times to count. Our experience with her was based on her terrific musical skills and great rapport with children. Little did we know she had a little "pirate" hiding inside.

Hales Miller is just amazing. Diver, Teacher, Mermaid! We were so lucky to cross paths with her and thankful that she agreed to share her story.

Nathan Richardson was gracious to give additional tips about what it takes to be a successful historic interpreter.

Tatiana Tchalabaeva is nothing short of magical. Always a smile. Always positive. I once asked legendary ringmaster Johnathan Lee Iverson, who had toured with her for years, if he had ever seen Tatiana without that smile. He said, "no." There could be no performer more perfect to ride a magical horse!

Laura Baldwin and Tony Gabriele are cherished members of the Rainbow family. We appreciate them for all they have contributed and continue to contribute.

David Haycox and Chris Mangune were so generous in sharing their photos.

Glossary

abolitionist – a person who wants to end slavery. John Brown and Frederick Douglass were abolitionists.

ambassador – a person who represents or promotes an idea, country, or business. "She is an ambassador for the Chesapeake Bay."

anesthesiologist – someone who monitors a patient's well-being before, during, and after surgery.

assassination – the murder of an important person. President Abraham Lincoln and President John F. Kennedy were assassinated.

bifocals – eyeglasses with two different lenses for each eye. Usually, one lens is for close up viewing and another for distance viewing.

devastating – destructive or damaging.

engineer – someone who designs or maintains a machine or structure.

extrasolar planet – a planet outside of our solar system.

fiberglass – a plastic, woven building material made from strands of glass.

Gettysburg Address – a speech given by Abraham Lincoln to dedicate the national cemetery at the site of the Battle of Gettysburg.

huckster - a person who sells or promotes something, usually of questionable value

historic interpreter – a person who portrays people from history.

narwhal – a small whale from the Arctic. The males have a twisted "tusk" created from one of its teeth.

paper-mâché – a modeling material made of paper pieces held together by glue or starch.

resins – a thick, liquid mixture of materials used for sculpting crafts, and other purposes.

Tuskegee Airmen - a famous group of African American pilots and support staff who fought in World War II.

Trademarks:

The use of the following trademarked names or images is for editorial purposes only and does not imply endorsement.

Grave Digger: Feld Motor Sports, Inc.

Jurassic Park: Amblin' Entertainment, Inc., Universal City Studios LLC

Kermit the Frog: The Muppets Studio, LLC

Maytag: Maytag Properties, LLC

Mythbusters: Discovery Communications, LLC

Ringling Brothers and Barnum & Bailey Circus: Ringling Bros.-Barnum & Bailey Combined Shows, Inc.

Tripadvisor: Tripadvisor, LLC

Universal Studios: Universal City Studios, Inc.

Bibliography

"How Florida's Seminole Tribe Transformed Alligator Wrestling into a Symbol of Independence," New Yorker Magazine Online, by Murat Oztaskin.
Accessed November 18, 2021

"Student Reporter Jaden Jefferson's Interview with Veteran Astronaut Alvin Drew," National Air and Space Museum YouTube video.
Accessed November 18, 2021

"Students Speak with Alvin Drew, Habitat Demo Unit Project Lead, Advanced Exploration Systems Program," NASA YouTube video.
Accessed November 12, 2021

Quotes from azquotes.com and goodreads.com.
Accessed November 26, 2021

David Messick is the founder of Rainbow Puppet Productions. He has written several children's books and dozens of original children's musicals that have been performed at the Smithsonian, New York's American Museum of Natural History, and many other organizations. He has also worked on development projects for the Oprah Winfrey Show and the Disney Channel and worked with many legendary performers. He and his wife Marcy are the parents of two amazing young men… Joshua and Luke.
http://davidmessick.com

Liu Light is an illustrator and multimedia designer in California. Light has illustrated a number of children's books with a focus on books featuring diverse voices and stories for such organizations as Shout Mouse Press and Rainbow Puppet Productions. Liu also enjoys drawing animations and comics.
http://liulight.com

Alvin Septiawan is a concept artist and illustrator from Indonesia. This is his first project with Rainbow Puppet Productions.

Other books from David and Liu:

The Amazing Adventures of Chessie the Manatee
Creatures Great and Small
Mary Peake and the Mighty Acorn
Never Give Up, Short Stories about Big Dreams
Open a Book
The Precarious Predicaments of Pinocchio
The Tall, the Tough, and the Tiny

Audio Programs from David and the Rainbow Puppets:

The Amazing Adventures of Chessie the Manatee
From the Sea to the Sky
Jonah
The Mother Goose Travelling Rock and Roll Show
A Pirate Party
The Really Big Dinosaur Show
Toyland!
The Wetland Revue
The Wright Brothers– See Us Fly!

Available at Amazon.com, RainbowPuppets.com, and DavidMessick.com